Peachtree City Library
201 Willowbend Road
Peachtree City, Ga. 30269

J
GUE_____
HILLARY RUDHAM
CLINTON A NEW KIND OF F
$10.13 PT 169715 C.06

NoLey 12/12

PEACHTREE CITY LIBRARY
201 Willowbend Road
Peachtree City, GA 30269

Hillary Rodham CLINTON

A New Kind of First Lady

JoAnn Bren Guernsey

Lerner Publications Company ▪ Minneapolis

FLINT RIVER REGIONAL LIBRARY

To the two young women who most inspire me—
my daughters Meghan and Jessica

ACKNOWLEDGMENTS: Arkansas Children's Hospital/Kelly Quinn, 55; Arkansas Democrat Gazette, 9, 46, 49, 52, 54; Mark Baldwin, 70; Douglas Chandor, White House Collection, 14; IPS, 32; Don Jones, 28; Dixie Knight, 65, 69; Harry Lerner, 38; David Lustbader, 35; Maine East High School, 18, 23; Maine South High School, 22, 26, 27, 72; Minneapolis Institute of Art, 30; Ernest Ricketts, 21 (top); Park Ridge Times Herald, 21 (bottom); Kelly Quinn, 2, 58; Reuters/Bettmann, 50, 62, 66, 67, 70, 74, 75; © Beverly Rezneck, 78; © Francis M. Roberts, 6, back cover; Karelle Scharff, 11; UPI, 33. Front cover photograph courtesy of the White House.

LIBRARY OF CONGRESS CATALOGING-IN-PUBLICATION DATA

Guernsey, JoAnn Bren.
 Hillary Rodham Clinton, a new kind of first lady/JoAnn Bren Guernsey.
  p. cm.–(The Achievers)
  Summary: A biography of Hillary Rodham Clinton, covering her personal background, her views on social issues, and her role in her husband's political career.
  ISBN 0-8225-2875-4 (lib. bdg.)
  ISBN 0-8225-9650-4 (pbk.)
  1. Clinton, Hillary Rodham—Juvenile literature.   2. Presidents—United States—Wives—Biography—Juvenile literature. [1. Clinton, Hillary Rodham. 2. First ladies.] I. Title. II. Series.
E887,C55G84   1993
973.929'092—dc20
[B]   93-21856
                                                                CIP
                                                                 AC

Copyright © 1993 by Lerner Publications Company

All rights reserved. International copyright secured. No part of this book may be reproduced or transmitted in any form or by any means, electronic or mechanical, including photocopying and recording, or by any information storage or retrieval system, without permission in writing from Lerner Publications Company, except for the inclusion of brief quotations in an acknowledged review.

Manufactured in the United States of America

International Standard Book Number: 0-8225-2875-4
Library of Congress Catalog Card Number: 93-21856

1 2 3 4 5 6 – P/JR – 98 97 96 95 94 93

Contents

Soon after Hillary Rodham Clinton became First Lady, she visited with children in a New York City school.

1
A Woman's Hand

Hillary Rodham Clinton, a small woman with blond hair and piercing blue eyes, stood before a classroom full of high school students. These gifted young people had been specially chosen as future leaders by the state of Arkansas. The boys weren't just raising their hands—they were practically leaping from their seats to be noticed. The girls were quiet and prim, sitting with their hands folded.

On that hot July day in 1992—just four months before her husband was elected president of the United States—Hillary Clinton gazed across the room, waiting. Finally, she said, "I'm looking for a woman's hand." She went on to assure the young women that, as a lawyer and a politician's wife, she understood why even the most liberated women sometimes hesitate to step forward. "There's that kind of double bind that women find themselves in," she said. "On the one hand, yes, be smart, stand up for yourself. On the other hand, don't offend anybody, don't step on toes, or you'll become somebody that nobody likes because you're too assertive."

Hillary understood this "double bind" all too well. During the months preceding her classroom visit, she'd been stung over and over again by the public and the media. People attacked almost everything about her—her successful career, her remarks to the media, and even the "preppy" headband she wore in her hair. The 1992 presidential campaign stirred more controversy about a candidate's *wife* than any previous campaign. Many newspapers and magazines, including the *New York Times*, *Newsweek*, and *Time*, wrote about the "Hillary Factor" and the "Hillary Problem."

Such personal attacks were difficult for Hillary, but they were not new to her. She'd spent over 20 years in a delicate balancing act, trying to be herself— intelligent and assertive—and wanting to be liked. When her husband, Bill, lost his 1980 bid for a second term as governor in his home state of Arkansas, many people blamed Hillary. The majority of voters in Arkansas didn't like women whom they considered "radical feminists."

In order to help her husband win the next election, Hillary allowed herself to be "made over." Ever since she was 16, Hillary had tried to wear contact lenses,

In 1980 the voters of Arkansas did not think that Hillary Rodham looked like a proper First Lady of their state.

but she couldn't get hard contact lenses to stay in her eyes. After Bill's 1980 defeat, Hillary got soft contact lenses to replace her thick glasses. She began using makeup, dyeing her hair blond, and wearing fashionable suits and dresses instead of the baggy sweaters she preferred. The biggest change, however, was giving up her maiden name. When Bill and Hillary were married, she had kept the last name of her family—Rodham—rather than changing it to Clinton. Before the 1982 campaign, Hillary Rodham became Hillary Rodham Clinton.

Bill Clinton won the 1982 election. Of course, he had also made many changes in his image and in his approach to the voters. But it is likely that he would have suffered another defeat with Hillary *Rodham* at his side instead of the new, quieter, more feminine-looking wife that Hillary Clinton had become.

Although she wished people would be more accepting of individual styles and differences among political wives, Hillary didn't regret doing what she could to help her husband become governor again. And her years in the political spotlight in Arkansas helped prepare her for what she experienced during the 1992 presidential campaign. Hillary tried not to take personally the criticism she and her husband received.

In many ways, Hillary's life mirrors those of other women who grew into adulthood during the turbulent 1960s, who perhaps got married, and perhaps launched careers during the 1970s. Many of them consider themselves feminists who believe in equality for women. During the 1992 presidential campaign, Hillary became a symbol of the changing roles of women in the 1990s, She became, in a sense, the spokeswoman for her generation—the "baby boomers"—those born in the years immediately following World War II.

Being a symbol of anything is indeed a burden, but friends and supporters of the Clintons believe that Hillary Rodham Clinton is up to the challenge. During

A more glamorous Hillary campaigned for her husband during the 1992 presidential election.

the 1992 campaign, she emerged as not only the wife of a promising young politician and the mother of 12-year-old Chelsea; she was also an extremely accomplished professional woman.

For years before the 1992 election, Hillary had been a top corporate lawyer and had served as a director on several corporate boards. Twice, the *National Law Journal* named her one of the 100 "most influential" lawyers in the country. She had provided the main financial support for her family, since she earned three to four times more money than her husband did as governor. She had also worked hard and effectively for better education and for children's rights.

Hillary can give an impressive 40-minute speech without notes, testify confidently before legislative committees, absorb huge amounts of information, ask all the right questions, and make persuasive arguments for change. In short, she gets things done. Even a conservative Arkansas journalist who strongly opposes everything about Bill Clinton admitted that "the best thing that could happen would be to let Hillary run the country. I know that sounds ridiculous, but she has just never failed."

In spite of her many gifts, Hillary is not intimidating in person—except perhaps in court. She loves movies and movie stars—Kevin Costner is a favorite. She enjoys playing games (such as Pictionary) and playing the piano (badly, she says). She admits that she's not much of a cook. She responds to jokes with a wonderful belly laugh and is always available for her friends. And she is a devoted mother to Chelsea.

So, what is the "problem" so many people had with Hillary? Would voters have felt more comfortable with Bill Clinton if he hadn't married someone so exceptional? The year 1992 was called the Year of the Woman because so many women were running for political office. Why, then, did it seem easier for a strong, independent woman to be a *candidate* than to be a candidate's *wife*?

The answer is probably that many Americans are still not certain about the role of women in society. Even as a symbol of change, Hillary was, according to some voters, a little *too* impressive. Could she fit comfortably into the role of First Lady—the president's wife? How would she shape and change the role? Would the role change her?

Most troubling to many people was the idea that Hillary might have too much control over decision making in the White House. It was, after all, her husband whom the voters had elected, not her.

Historically, First Ladies have served primarily as official hostesses and have presented the picture of a traditional wife and mother. They have often supported special projects or causes, but these projects have typically involved work defined by men as

Eleanor Roosevelt became First Lady in 1933.

appropriate for women. First Ladies have usually remained relatively quiet in public. Lou Henry Hoover (wife of President Herbert Hoover) had worked with her husband on translating a book about mining before he was elected, and she wrote articles for scientific and historical publications. But a First Lady with a professional career and a long list of accomplishments separate and distinct from those of her husband had never moved into the White House. Many First Ladies have come to the White House while raising children, but Hillary Rodham Clinton became the first First Lady to carry out her duties as a mother, the formal White House duties expected of her, *and* professional duties.

Mrs. Clinton has often pointed to Eleanor Roosevelt, the wife of President Franklin Delano Roosevelt, as a role model. Mrs. Roosevelt became famous during the 1930s and 1940s as a social activist—a person who feels strongly enough about people and issues to take action on their behalf. Her special causes included youth employment, civil rights for minorities, and international human rights. Mrs. Roosevelt, however, began her career only after moving into the White House. She traveled nationwide on lecture tours, held press conferences, and wrote a daily newspaper column. And she suffered harsh criticism for her activism.

First Ladies of the late 20th century have found themselves in situations similar to Eleanor Roosevelt's. Lady Bird Johnson made beautification of the country her special cause—hardly controversial, yet she was often criticized for her efforts. Rosalynn Carter was criticized for sitting in on cabinet meetings, high-level meetings of presidential advisers. Nancy Reagan had the habit of prompting her husband and finishing his sentences. Many people thought such behavior was too pushy. Perhaps Martha Washington, America's first First Lady, described the position best. She said, "I am more like a state prisoner than anything else."

During the 1992 campaign, Hillary frequently found herself being compared to Barbara Bush, who was First Lady at that time. Mrs. Bush had a grandmotherly appearance, and she symbolized the traditional supporting role of women. "I don't think we ought to move from one stereotype of a First Lady to another," Hillary said. "I admire Barbara Bush and all the women who have found themselves in that position, who have tried to shape the position to their needs and their husbands' needs. The choices a woman makes should be respected."

"The choices a woman makes"—this is, perhaps, the phrase that most clearly defines feminism for Hillary and many other women. Thirty years ago, women had fewer choices. Most women stayed home to take care of their homes and families. During the 1970s and 1980s, however, more and more women began to pursue careers outside the home. Even for those women who chose to make homemaking their career, the troubled economy made it difficult for families to live on only one parent's income. In addition, more and more marriages ended in divorce, and single mothers had to support themselves and their children.

By the 1990s, most women with children expected to work outside the home, either as part of a two-career family or as a single parent. In 1992 the Clintons asked the people of the United States to accept a First Lady who had a career of her own. At the beginning of the presidential campaign, Bill Clinton proudly advertised himself and Hillary as a "buy one, get one free" bargain. They were surprised by the negative reaction that approach drew from the public and from some people within the government. They soon backed away from any hint that Hillary might be too directly involved in a Clinton administration.

During the campaign, former president Richard Nixon expressed the common belief that a strong wife "makes her husband look like a wimp." Nixon also said, "Hillary pounds the piano so hard that Bill can't be heard. You want a wife who's intelligent, but not too intelligent."

Many people, especially feminists, are frustrated by this kind of statement. They say that Bill Clinton, rather than appearing weak in comparison to Hillary, is living proof that it takes a solid, secure man to marry a strong woman.

Eleanor McGovern, wife of former presidential candidate George McGovern, said she'd been given a hard time during her husband's campaign for being a children's advocate and for being "too serious." She became a strong Hillary Clinton supporter and couldn't understand all the Hillary-bashing. "You get two capable people in government," McGovern said. "You should be able to use their abilities to the utmost. Someone has to make the break, and Hillary's the one."

Hillary, *standing,* was vice president of her junior class.

2
A Young Activist

Hillary Diane Rodham was born on October 26, 1947, at Edgewater Hospital on the north side of Chicago. She grew up in a stone and brick house on the corner of Wisner and Elm streets in Park Ridge, Illinois, a middle-class suburb of Chicago. Her father, Hugh Rodham, started out as a curtain salesman at the Columbia Lace Company and then ran his own drapery-making business in Chicago for 30 years. Dorothy Howell Rodham, Hillary's mother, met Hugh when she applied for a secretarial job at the lace company in 1937. Dorothy and Hugh were married in 1942.

Dorothy stayed home to raise Hillary and her two younger brothers, Hugh and Tony. She was proud of her full-time occupation as housewife and mother. At the same time, she developed and passed on to her children what would later be considered feminist ideals. She said, "I was determined that no daughter of mine was going to have to go through the agony of being afraid to say what she had on her mind."

Hillary learned early in life to assert herself. A family in her neighborhood had a child named Suzy, who bullied other children. Hillary was a small four-year-old with ribbons in her hair when she became the frequent target of Suzy's fists. After being hit, Hillary would run home sobbing. One day her mother made an announcement: "There's no room in this house for cowards. You're going to have to stand up to her."

It wasn't long before Hillary faced Suzy again, and the two girls soon attracted a circle of curious boys. Nobody expected what happened next. Hillary—eyes closed—threw out her fist, knocking Suzy to the ground. The boys' mouths dropped open in awe. Hillary raced home, flushed with her triumph, and exclaimed to her mother that she was now tough enough to "play with the boys."

Hillary quickly became a natural leader in the neighborhood. "She just took charge," her mother recalls. But Hillary wasn't interested in having power over others for the sake of power. She was intent on action, especially action aimed at helping other people. After becoming involved in one cause or another, she would motivate other children to join her.

The Rodham house in Park Ridge, Illinois

In her sixth grade class photo, Hillary sits at the far right in the bottom row.

At one point, for example, she became concerned about the children of Mexican migrant workers who picked crops on farms near her home. (Migrant families travel from farm to farm seeking work. Their pay is low, and their living conditions are meager.) To raise money and gather clothing for these migrant workers, Hillary organized neighborhood carnivals and sports tournaments. Later, she was also involved in a baby-sitting service for the migrant children.

In her senior year of high school, Hillary, *far left in the bottom row,* was a National Merit Scholarship finalist, *left.* At Maine East, she also served on the sportsmanship committee, *opposite page, third from left in the bottom row.*

Early in her life, in other words, she became an activist. She led a privileged life, and she felt that she owed something to other children who weren't as lucky as she was.

Hillary valued her supportive family and the full range of opportunities offered to her. When she was in sixth grade, she took piano lessons from Margaret-Lucy Lessard, whose house was just down the street from the Rodhams'. Hillary also took ballet and played softball and volleyball. She was a Brownie and then a Girl Scout who earned almost every merit badge possible. But the Rodham children were not pampered. Their father had grown up during the Great Depression of the 1930s, and he insisted that his children learn about hardship and responsibility.

Hillary's brother Tony recalls, "We were probably the only kids in the whole suburb who didn't get an allowance. We'd rake the leaves, cut the grass, pull weeds, shovel snow. All your friends would be going to a movie. After your errands, you'd walk in and say, 'Gee, Dad, I could use two or three dollars.' He'd flop another potato on your dinner plate and say, 'That's your reward.'"

The biggest responsibility for the Rodham children was not chores, however; it was schoolwork. Hillary came home with A's from Eugene Field Elementary School, Emerson Junior High, Maine East High School, and again in her senior year from the newly built Maine South. Elisabeth King, known as a strict teacher, was one of Hillary's favorites in both elementary school and junior high.

Hillary's parents expected great things from her, and her brothers had to follow her trail of academic excellence and DAR (Daughters of the American Revolution) community service awards. Her mother had hoped that Hillary would be the first woman on the Supreme Court, but Sandra Day O'Connor beat her to it in 1981. Hillary's father was extremely demanding. At report card time, Hillary remembers her mother saying, "Oh, that's wonderful, dear," while her father would say, "You must go to a pretty easy school."

Her mother says that she "explained to Hillary very early that school was a great adventure, that she was going to learn great things, live new passions. . . . Maybe that's why Hillary was never afraid. Not of school. Not of anything."

Like most of the children in Park Ridge, Hillary went to see movies at the Pickwick Theater and to Ted and Pearl's Happy House for Cokes. But she had a serious side too. When she was 14 years old, Hillary wrote to the National Aeronautics and Space Administration (NASA) to ask what she had to do to become an astronaut. The response from NASA told her that they "weren't taking any girls." She recalls being furious. Later, she calmed down somewhat, realizing that "I couldn't have been an astronaut anyway, because I have such terrible eyesight."

Competitive sports also played an important role in shaping young Hillary's character. She was not a gifted athlete, but she participated with enthusiasm anyway. In those days, athletic teams were almost entirely for boys. Hillary now appreciates the lessons few other girls her age had the chance to learn from sports. "You win one day, you lose the next day, you don't take it personally. You get up every day and you go on."

Perhaps the most important influence during her youth, however, came from the First United Methodist Church, a red brick building not far from the Rodham house. When Hillary was in ninth grade, the Reverend Donald Jones arrived from New York City to become the new youth minister. It wasn't until he arrived that Hillary felt she truly understood the teachings of her church. Kids called his Thursday night class the "University of Life." Jones talked about God, war, violence, art—about real life. Since all of the teenagers in the youth group were white and middle-class, Jones

Hillary, *second from left in the middle row,* was a member of the first student council at Maine South during her senior year.

Hillary, *second from left in the top row,* was a star on the debate team at Maine South High School.

took them on trips to a youth center on Chicago's South Side to meet and talk with street kids, gang members, blacks, and Hispanics.

Together, Donald Jones and the young people from various backgrounds talked about ways in which each individual can actually make a difference in the world. And together, in 1962, they went to hear civil rights leader Dr. Martin Luther King, Jr., speak. After the speech, Jones took his youth group backstage, and one by one, introduced the teenagers to Dr. King.

The church group was especially important to Hillary because she was growing up and attending school in a white, conservative neighborhood, sheltered from the troubled world outside Park Ridge, Illinois.

Hillary was an excellent student, but as she grew older and more confident, she noticed something about her high school that bothered her. She has said, "I saw a lot of my friends who had been really lively and smart and doing well in school beginning to worry that boys would think they were *too* smart, or beginning to cut back on how well they did or the courses they took, because that's not where their boyfriends were." To Hillary this made no sense, and she resisted the pressure to conform.

Did her impressive accomplishments at school—top grades, student council activities, debate team stardom—make her unpopular? Not at all.

The Reverend Donald Jones had a major impact on the lives of Hillary and her high school friends.

"Boys liked her," the Reverend Donald Jones says. "And not because she was flirtatious. She was not—she wasn't a raving beauty, but she was pretty enough. What attracted guys around her was her personality, her willingness to talk to them." He also recalls that Hillary "wasn't going to take a backseat to anyone. She wouldn't let some young man dominate meetings if he had nothing to say."

During Hillary's senior year in high school, she worked for the Barry Goldwater presidential campaign and wore a sash that said "Goldwater Girl." As a member of the student council, she organized a mock political convention in the gym with posters, podiums, and nominating speeches.

That same year, Hillary and seven girlfriends rented a station wagon and drove to Pompano Beach, Florida, during spring break. Hillary graduated from high school in 1965 with many honors, including a social-science award.

By that time, Hillary knew that she had been accepted at Wellesley College, an excellent women's college near Boston, Massachusetts. She had also considered Smith and Radcliffe colleges, but when she saw pictures of the beautiful Wellesley campus, she made her decision. Wellesley offered challenge and adventure. Even Hillary was intimidated by Wellesley at first—but not for long.

Robert Rauschenberg's silk screen, *Signs,* depicts the turbulence of the 1960s, during which Hillary attended Wellesley College.

3
Campus Leader

Hugh Rodham drove his wife and daughter from Park Ridge, Illinois, to Wellesley, Massachusetts, in his Cadillac, the type of car he always drove. Hughie and Tony were left at home with a baby-sitter.

The four years (1965–1969) during which Hillary attended Wellesley were amazing years to be in college. It was a time of great turbulence. Malcolm X (the leader of a movement to unite black people) was assassinated in 1965. Civil rights leader Martin Luther King, Jr., was assassinated in April 1968. And Robert F. Kennedy (who was seeking the presidential nomination of the Democratic party) was assassinated in June 1968. Many American cities, including Chicago, were scarred by riots following King's death. The Vietnam War raged on and so did protest against it. Protest against this unpopular war was especially

College students throughout the nation protested against U.S. participation in the Vietnam War.

strong on college campuses. "We were in school when everything seemed to be falling apart at the seams," says one of Hillary's Wellesley friends, Kris Olson Rogers. "And the campus often reflected the unrest in society at large."

During their summer vacation in August 1968, Hillary and her friend Betsy Johnson Ebeling took the train from Park Ridge to downtown Chicago, where the Democratic National Convention was taking place. They wanted to see the thousands of demonstrators who had assembled in Grant Park to protest against U.S. involvement in the Vietnam War. They were not

During the 1968 Democratic National Convention in Chicago, Illinois, police battled antiwar demonstrators. Blood runs down the neck of this wounded demonstrator.

prepared for what they saw. "We saw kids our age getting their heads beaten in. And the police were doing the beating," said Ebeling. "We had had a wonderful childhood in Park Ridge, but we obviously hadn't gotten the whole story."

Hillary majored in political science and also studied psychology. Many of her professors were deeply involved in the civil rights and antiwar movements. Her political views had already become more liberal than those of her parents, who were staunch Republicans. But she was still a Republican during her first year at Wellesley.

Over the next few years, however, Hillary gradually decided that she was a Democrat. She became more and more outspoken about campus reform as well as wider issues such as the war. She organized the first anti-Vietnam War protest at Wellesley College. Often, she drew upon her gifts as a natural leader and her talent for bridging the gap between different groups. Kris Olson Rogers says that Hillary "was the one who was always giving speeches, calling meetings, making things happen." But her sense of humor, her compassion, and her down-to-earth nature made her well liked no matter how pushy or opinionated she might otherwise have seemed.

During her sophomore year, Hillary and several other students tried to get Wellesley to increase its enrollment of black students. According to classmate Jan Piercy, "We were all still afraid to talk about it. But Hillary's attitude was, 'What's so embarrassing? If we're not willing to talk about it, how are we going to get past it? If prejudice exists, let's talk about it.'"

In addition to her studies, Hillary often drove into the Roxbury section of Boston, where she helped to teach poor children to read and worked for increased voting access for minorities. Naturally, her unique brand of activism did alienate some people. At least one classmate remembers Hillary's strong personality as "not everyone's cup of tea."

After her graduation ceremony, Hillary took a swim in Lake Waban on the Wellesley College campus.

On campus she protested against curfews, the ban on men being in the dormitories, and certain required classes. Just like other students, she dated and loved to dance—especially to the sounds of Motown. She also loved endless hours of spirited debate. Her former child psychology professor, Patsy Sampson, remembers Hillary as "intense and very serious."

Hillary was elected president of her college government and graduated in 1969 with high honors. She was the first graduating senior ever to give a commencement address at Wellesley. Combining her own ideas with those of her classmates, she delivered a speech that sharply criticized the administration of President Nixon. Her words were eloquent, yet practical, in their call to action. "The challenge now is to practice politics as the art of making what appears to be impossible, possible." *Life* magazine featured an article about her along with her photograph.

After her graduation ceremonies ended, Hillary celebrated by swimming in Lake Waban, a lake on the Wellesley campus. Swimming was prohibited except at the beach, but that was one of the rules that Hillary often broke. She stripped down to her swimming suit, put her clothes and her "Coke-bottle" glasses in a pile, and waded in just off Tupelo Point. While she was paddling around, a security guard came by, picked up the pile of clothes and her glasses, and carried them off. Years later she told the Wellesley class of 1992, "Imagine my surprise when I emerged to find neither clothes nor glasses, and, blind as a bat, I had to feel my way back to Stone-Davis [her dormitory]."

After Wellesley, Hillary decided to go to law school, but not with an eye toward the wealth and privilege sought by many of her classmates. She chose law school as a means of being socially useful. She rejected Harvard because one of the professors there coldly informed her that "we don't need any more women." Instead, Hillary chose Yale.

In the spring of her first year at law school, Hillary heard Marian Wright Edelman, founder of the Children's Defense Fund (CDF), speak on campus. CDF is a group that attends to some of the urgent needs of children—needs such as health care and day care. It was partly because of this group and its founder that Hillary developed an intense interest in children's issues. Hillary had read about Edelman earlier in *Time* magazine. After hearing her speak, however, Hillary decided she wanted to spend her summer working for Edelman. Because CDF had no money to hire Hillary, she found her own financing. That summer of 1970 marked the beginning of Hillary's ongoing involvement with the law and children.

Hillary had been one of only 30 women to enter Yale Law School in 1969, and 10 of the other women soon dropped out. Many of the professors and male students resented the women at Yale and told them they were taking the places of more "worthy" men who were off fighting and dying in Vietnam.

Fortunately for Hillary, not all the men at Yale felt threatened by strong, intelligent women. In the fall of 1970, a young man arrived on campus after studying at Oxford University in England. He, in particular, appreciated her strengths. He was a tall, charming Arkansan named William Jefferson Clinton.

Yale University features beautiful Gothic architecture.

4
From Yale to Arkansas

Bill Clinton was talking with a friend in the Yale Law School Library when he was distracted. A young woman wearing a flannel shirt and thick glasses was sitting at the other end of the room reading. He couldn't stop staring at her. When she looked up from her book, she noticed him watching her, and she stared back. Finally, she shut her book, walked down to where Bill sat and said, "Look, if you're going to keep staring at me, and I'm going to keep staring back, I think we should at least introduce ourselves. I'm Hillary Rodham. What's your name?"

Completely taken by surprise, Bill, for a moment, forgot his name. "I was embarrassed," he says now. "It turned out she knew who I was. But I was really impressed, and we've been together, more or less, ever since."

Hillary presents an effective case in a mock trial.

Hillary had already asked her friends about the outgoing young southerner. She'd heard a man bragging about his Arkansas roots in the student lounge one day. "And not only that," she heard him say, "we have the largest watermelons in the world!" She thought he was handsome and intriguing. But when asked years later what attracted her to Bill, Hillary said, "He wasn't afraid of me."

Bill had a feeling from the start that Hillary would be an important part of his life. They began spending time together both on and off campus. Susan Bucknell, a friend of theirs at the time, recalls how much fun it was to be with them. "They enjoyed and respected each other. As women grappling with the Women's Movement, and as young women trained for professional careers, we were searching for men who would support and respect our potential. I always felt that Bill and Hillary had a solid foundation for an equal partnership. I had a sense that this was a couple who would have made it across the West in a covered wagon."

Don Pogue says that Clinton, his former roommate, was most attracted by "awesome intellect," both in professors and in other students, especially in Hillary. "People who think Hillary is smart," Pogue says, "are like people who think Shakespeare is a good writer."

Hillary's former classmates at Yale describe her as studious, solemn, dynamic, direct, and outspoken. She gave practically no thought to her hair or makeup. Bill was funny, gracious, and easy to like. He was, however, just as intense as Hillary, and perhaps even more ambitious. He warned her from the beginning that their romance might be risky for her. She had a promising future as a big-city attorney or even as a political candidate herself. But his mind was already made up about politics and about serving the people of Arkansas. "I've got to go home," he told her. "It's just who I am."

They were both excellent students—getting A's on final exams, even when their political activities kept them from attending all their classes. But of the two, Hillary had the more organized and disciplined mind.

During the summer and fall of 1972, Bill and Hillary both moved to Texas to work for the Democratic presidential campaign of Senator George McGovern. Hillary worked in San Antonio to register Hispanic voters. Bill ran McGovern's state campaign headquarters in Austin. The experience proved to be valuable for them both, teaching them, among other things, some of the best ways to build political support.

Hillary would have graduated from law school a year before Bill Clinton, but she spent a fourth year studying at the Yale Child Study Center and doing research on the legal rights of children. In an article published in the *Harvard Educational Review*, she argued that children over 12 years old, in some instances, demonstrate an ability to make more responsible decisions about their lives than the adults raising them.

After graduating from Yale in 1973, Bill Clinton returned to Arkansas. He taught at the University of Arkansas Law School in Fayetteville and began work on his first political campaign. He ran for Congress in 1974 and almost won, in spite of his youth. Hillary worked in Cambridge, Massachusetts, as a staff attorney for the Children's Defense Fund. Although she took a new job within six months, her dedication to and work with the Children's Defense Fund continued for years.

Hillary's new job in Washington, D.C., was an exciting one. In January 1974, she became part of the legal staff for the House Judiciary Committee's impeachment inquiry—the committee that investigated President Richard Nixon's role in the Watergate scandal. The Watergate scandal involved burglary, wiretapping, sabotage, and an attempted cover-up of those actions. (The name *Watergate* comes from the Watergate complex of apartment and office buildings where the burglary took place.) Nixon and several members of his administration were part of a high-level cover-up of this criminal activity.

The committee's goal was to gather evidence that could impeach Nixon—in other words, charge him with a crime against the country. The work was thrilling because everyone involved knew they were part of a historic case. It was also exhausting. Hillary's life consisted of 18-hour workdays, haphazard meals, and late-night phone calls to Bill Clinton. In August, before the full case could be brought against him, Nixon resigned from the presidency. He knew that the American people had lost faith in him.

When her job in Washington, D.C., ended, Hillary sifted through job offers from law firms in Washington, New York, and Chicago. She knew she was at a critical point in her career. Finally Hillary made a difficult decision—one that shocked and dismayed her friends. She decided to move to Arkansas.

While living in Washington, Hillary had stayed with Sara Ehrmann, whom she had met while working on the McGovern campaign in Texas. Sara drove her, along with 20 boxes of books and a 10-speed bike, to Arkansas. Sara spent the whole 30-hour ride trying to talk Hillary out of the move. In Washington, Hillary had been in the middle of everything, on the edge of everything. Sara told Hillary, "You have the world at your feet. Why are you throwing your life away for this guy?"

But Hillary did not change her mind. Many of her friends asked her why she would move to Arkansas, a dirt-poor state with a total population of about one-quarter that of New York City. She responded by telling them she needed to get away from Washington, that her work there had been intense and exhausting, and that she had found Arkansas beautiful when she'd visited the state with Bill. But often her answer was simply, "I love him."

Bill was teaching at the University of Arkansas Law School in Fayetteville. Hillary decided to accept a job teaching criminal law at the same university. In addition, she set up the university's first program to provide legal services for people who cannot afford a lawyer.

Hillary loved Fayetteville, a small college town in the Ozark Mountains with hilly, tree-lined streets and lovely Victorian houses. Hillary lived and worked there for a year while trying to figure out whether she and Bill could build a life together.

In August 1975, Hillary left Fayetteville to visit friends who were still trying to change her mind about living in Arkansas. She went to Boston, New York, Washington, D.C., and Chicago. "I didn't see anything out there," she recalls, "that I thought was more exciting or challenging than what I had in front of me."

When Hillary returned, Bill picked her up at the Fayetteville airport. But instead of taking her to her apartment, he drove up to an unfamiliar house and stopped the car. He said, "I've bought that house you like."

"What house I like?"

"You know. Remember when we were driving around the day before you left and there was a 'For Sale' sign and you said, 'Gee, that's a nice house.'"

"Bill, that's all I said. I've never been inside it."

"Well, I thought you liked it, so I bought it. So I guess we'll have to get married now."

Two months later, in October 1975, they did.

Hillary stands beside her husband as he is sworn in as governor in 1979.

5
First Lady of Arkansas

Before the wedding, Bill and Hillary rounded up some friends to help paint the house he had bought as a surprise. "We had a wonderful life there," Hillary recalls. "The pace of life was so much slower, so much more open to long conversations with friends and dinners that went on for hours where you talked about everything that was going on in your life and in the world. I miss that in our lives now."

The pace soon picked up. Within a year, in 1976, Bill had been elected attorney general, and the couple moved to the capital city of Little Rock. For Hillary, living in Arkansas—especially as a political wife—was sometimes difficult. Even in the larger city of Little Rock, women were generally expected to focus on fashion and makeup, decorating their homes, and raising their families.

Did Hillary fit in? Not exactly. She didn't pay much attention to fashion, and she wanted to continue her law career. She became one of the first women in the state to join a major law office. The Rose Law Firm, highly respected in Arkansas and nationwide, asked Hillary to join them. Many of the firm's top lawyers had been impressed by her work at the university's legal-aid clinic.

Hillary quickly became known as an energetic and determined lawyer. Another lawyer in the law firm, Webb Hubbell, said, "I think initially there were some [clients] who might [have] put her into a stereotype... the pushy, Yankee female, but I don't think anybody after 15 minutes with Hillary would think that." She won respect as an attorney within the firm and as an activist within the community.

This situation changed dramatically in 1978 when Bill Clinton was elected governor. He was only 32 years old, and many people called him "the boy governor." Hillary and Bill were stunned that his political career was moving along so quickly. A close friend remembers the Clintons' first night in the governor's mansion. They were wandering throughout the enormous rooms, eating chocolate chip cookies, and quietly repeating the question, "Are we really here?"

Many older, more traditional Arkansas citizens wished that the young couple weren't there. Hillary, who continued to work at the law firm, became the

As First Lady of Arkansas, Hillary took a special interest in the quality of education.

focus of most of the criticism. With her thick glasses, shapeless sweaters, and her refusal to wear makeup, she did not *look* like the First Lady of Arkansas. Worst of all, she had kept her family name—Rodham—rather than changing her name to Clinton when she married Bill. Many Arkansans wanted a more decorative and eager-to-please First Lady. Instead, at the age of 32, Hillary became a partner at the Rose Law Firm.

The Clintons, Bill, Chelsea, and Hillary, in 1980

On February 17, 1980, Hillary gave birth to a baby girl. Chelsea was born prematurely, but she was healthy and weighed slightly over six pounds. The Clintons were thrilled with their "perfect child." However, when the newspapers reported that "Governor Bill *Clinton* and Hillary *Rodham* had a daughter," the citizens of Arkansas were outraged at what many considered too bold a display of feminism. The majority of Arkansans thought the announcement should have read "Governor and Mrs. Bill Clinton." Unfortunately, 1980 was an election year, and voters registered their disapproval.

Bill lost the election after having been governor for only one two-year term. He was devastated, and many experts predicted that his political career was over. "There are a couple of periods in my adult life that were pretty tough," he has said. At the backyard barbecue to say good-bye to his staff and thank supporters, both Bill and Hillary walked around teary-eyed. However, it was Hillary who finally pulled herself together and gave the thank-you speech.

The Clintons' marriage suffered after Bill lost the election, partly because the loss occurred just when Hillary's own career was soaring. Bill was happy for her success, but he himself felt like a failure. According to friends, he "went a little crazy." He became obsessed with his defeat and traveled all over the state asking people what he had done wrong. It was during this time that tales began to spread about Bill Clinton being a "womanizer." He became careless about his attention to and from some of the women who were attracted to the handsome young politician.

Hillary also took her husband's defeat hard and was frightened by the changes in Bill's behavior. During this dark period, she decided to do whatever it took to help Bill regain the governorship. Without even telling him first, she changed her last name to Clinton. Hillary was also willing to change something else that she hadn't cared much about—the way she looked.

The "new" Hillary in her 1983 inaugural gown

Together Bill and Hillary began to campaign nonstop, and it soon became clear how much help Hillary could be to Bill. She sat in on planning sessions and supported and pushed him when he grew discouraged or tired. And she did a great job of convincing voters to accept his ideas and plans for the government.

When Bill was reelected in 1982, one of the first appointments he made was that of chairperson for the state's new Arkansas Education Standards Committee. He appointed Hillary. The committee's job was to set standards for the quality of education throughout the state. Hillary traveled all over Arkansas to hold hearings and meet with groups of parents and teachers. In the end, the committee recommended some very drastic changes, including a law that would take away a high school student's driver's license if he or she dropped out of school. The committee also pushed for higher taxes and required tests for teachers to prove their ability to teach.

Bill Bowen, a Little Rock friend, believes that if Hillary had not changed her image from liberal feminist lawyer to traditional wife, she would not have been able to overhaul Arkansas's public schools. "If she had not learned to fit in," Bowen said, "she would never have enjoyed the same success. We all tend to listen to people who are like us, dress like us, don't put on airs."

Governor Clinton felt strongly about improving education in Arkansas. He supported the changes Hillary proposed, although they were extremely unpopular with teachers. Once again Hillary became the target of sharp attacks because she had chaired the committee responsible for the changes. Governor Clinton did not back down, however, and many statistics show that the improvement in Arkansas's education system has been one of the most dramatic in the country.

Over the years, Hillary also established the Home Instruction Program for Pre-School Youth, which helps teach low-income parents how to prepare their children for kindergarten. In addition, she set up the first neonatal-care nursery (hospital treatment of

As chairperson of the Arkansas Education Standards Committee, Hillary held hearings, met with students and teachers, and reported back to the legislature.

Hillary visits the neonatal-care nursery that she helped set up in Arkansas Children's Hospital.

newborns) and brought two fully equipped hospital helicopters to Arkansas. All the while, she dressed fashionably, and she hosted and attended the teas and luncheons expected of the governor's wife.

Since the late 1970s, Hillary had been a strong supporter of children's rights. She was one of the guiding forces in the Children's Defense Fund, the organization that had first hired her when she was still in law school. She and Governor Clinton both attended an important national meeting about education. At one point, Hillary sat next to President George Bush and took the opportunity to speak to him urgently about children's issues. She gave him statistics that ranked the United States below 16 other countries in preventing babies from dying within their first year.

"Well, Hillary," President Bush replied, "whatever are you talking about? Our health care system is the envy of the world."

"Well, not if you want to keep your child alive to the year of his first birthday," Hillary shot back. She encouraged him to look into the matter.

The next day, President Bush handed a note to Governor Clinton, saying, "Tell Hillary she was right."

Meanwhile, both Hillary and Bill tried to be the best possible parents to Chelsea—which wasn't always easy. Chelsea has spent a lot of time in the care of baby-sitters and nannies, but she has also been given the closest thing to a "normal" upbringing that the Clintons could manage. Bill and Hillary have both been dedicated, active parents, who rarely missed Chelsea's softball games or ballet recitals. They have helped her with homework and are there to untangle difficulties.

From the time she was little, Chelsea learned how important it is to care about people less fortunate than herself. Even as a young girl, she paid many visits to and spent several holidays at various shelters for the homeless and for battered women and their children. Most people agree that Chelsea is a bright, thoughtful, remarkable young woman.

In 1987 Bill Clinton was 40 years old and began to ready himself for a possible presidential campaign. After he and Hillary discussed the idea carefully, however, they decided it was too soon. They knew he would suffer negative publicity about affairs with other women, and Chelsea was too young to be exposed to the difficulties and possible ugliness of such a campaign. When Bill announced to the press his decision not to run, Hillary stood behind him in tears. To the public, it was a rare glimpse of her emotions.

Four years later, Bill had been governor of Arkansas for almost a decade, and they both were ready for a change and a challenge. So, one morning in August of 1991, Hillary woke up and peered into her husband's sleepy face. "You almost *have* to do it," she said— meaning run for president of the United States.

"Do you have any idea what we're getting into?" he asked.

"I know, it'll be tough," was her answer. But neither of them were quite prepared for just how tough it would be.

The Clintons on election night, 1992

6
Two Candidates for the Price of One

During Bill Clinton's 1990 campaign for a fifth term as governor, his opponent, Tom McCrae, held a press conference while the governor was out of town. McCrae's attacks on the governor had barely begun before another voice interrupted. The cameras swung to the pale blond woman who had placed herself opposite McCrae. "Tom, give me a break! I think we oughta set the record straight."

Hillary Clinton displayed and read from reports McCrae himself had written, which highly praised Governor Clinton's achievements. "For goodness sake," she said, "let Arkansas stand up and be proud. We've made more progress than any other state except South Carolina and we're right up there with them." Tom McCrae, who eventually lost to Bill Clinton, looked embarrassed and stunned.

A year later, Hillary took an active role in her husband's campaign for the presidency. The journey from candidacy to presidency proved to be difficult and exhausting. Hillary often appeared to be tense. She sometimes seemed to be enjoying herself much less than Governor Clinton, the natural politician. But when she was playing a strong, vocal role in the campaign, the passion in her words and the impact of her presence was impossible to miss.

Patricia Derian, an assistant secretary of state during President Jimmy Carter's administration, saw Hillary at a benefit in Washington and commented, "The *instant* she came in the door of the ballroom, I knew it." No spotlight lit her way, no music announced her, and Hillary was barely taller than the podium microphone. "But there was no missing her, and that's really rare. She's a spectacular candidate in her own right."

Bill never hesitates to join in the praise. "I've always liked strong women," he says. "It doesn't bother me for people to see her and get excited and say she could be president. I always say she could be president, too."

But not everyone admired Hillary during the campaign. Many accused her of trying to steal the spotlight from her husband. After Clinton's victory in the Illinois primary, for example, when the television networks wanted to tape his reaction, Hillary's introduction of her husband turned into a speech of her own while he stood in the background. Interviewing her could be frustrating at times also. Unlike her husband, she did not like to sit and chat, nor did she reveal much about herself. Reporters often got the impression that Hillary felt that she had to answer their questions, but she didn't have to like doing so.

The biggest challenge to the Clinton campaign came in January 1992. The stories about the governor's involvement with other women had surfaced and spread by that time. Attacks on him grew most intense after a woman named Gennifer Flowers claimed to have had a 12-year affair with Governor Clinton. Of course, this period of time was painful for Hillary. She was especially worried about how Chelsea might react, even though she had been warned long before the campaign that she would hear "people say some bad things about Daddy."

In a joint interview on the television show *60 Minutes*, Hillary and Bill sat side by side defending their marriage. They also had to defend his candidacy. Bill came across as sincere and admitted that he'd made some personal mistakes in the past. But he also said that he'd learned from them and was totally devoted to his family.

During the interview, Hillary's presence was strong, and she often jumped in to see that the interview stayed focused. At one point she said, "I'm sitting here because I love him and I respect him and I honor what he's been through and what we've been

Hillary joins her husband for an early-morning jog on the beach at Hilton Head, South Carolina.

through together. If that's not enough for people, then heck, don't vote for him."

Voters liked what they saw—a couple struggling to keep their marriage going, but not willing to bow too much to public pressure. The interview went a long way toward saving Bill's candidacy. Everyone involved in the campaign heaved a sigh of relief. And what did

Chelsea think? When she watched the taped program together with her mother and father, she said, "I think I'm glad you're my parents."

During this low point in the campaign, Bill and Chelsea planned to attend a father-daughter dance at the Little Rock Y.W.C.A. They were both looking forward to it as a much-needed escape from public life. Many people involved in his campaign thought the dance would be a perfect photo opportunity to boost Bill's image as a devoted father. Long before campaign workers could notify the press, however, Hillary said, "No. This is Chelsea's night."

But shielding Chelsea and supporting Bill weren't Hillary's only challenges during the campaign. There was, after all, the "Hillary Problem."

The worst criticism of her probably followed a snappish remark she made in March 1992 that offended millions of women. Governor Jerry Brown, one of Clinton's opponents during the primary campaign, attacked Hillary's career. In response, Hillary said to reporters, "I suppose I could have stayed home and baked cookies and had teas, but what I decided to do was fulfill my profession, which I entered before my husband was in public life."

These words were repeated over and over in newspapers and on television. She had gone on to say, "The work that I have done as a professional, a public advocate, has been aimed ... to assure that women can make the choices . . . whether it's a full-time career, full-time motherhood, or some combination." Only the "cookies" comment made the news though, and it appeared to belittle homemakers. It also seemed to show an insensitive, thoughtless side of Hillary.

Hillary was surprised and frustrated by the way her words were interpreted. She learned a difficult lesson about the way the media can take small parts of a speech and distort the speaker's whole point of view. "I've learned to be more careful in what I say," she commented in an interview shortly before the election, "because I really don't mind having people disagree with me so long as they are disagreeing with what I really believe or say."

Another controversy that arose during the campaign centered around Hillary's legal writings during the 1970s about children's rights. She was concerned about giving children a legal way out of abusive or negligent families. She wrote that teenagers should be treated more like adults, and that parents should not, by themselves, have authority to make "decisions about motherhood and abortion, schooling, cosmetic surgery, treatment of venereal disease, or employment." When opponents dug up these legal articles, they distorted them to make Hillary look like a radical who encouraged children to sue their parents over every dispute from allowances to taking out the garbage.

Hillary speaks at a homecoming rally in Little Rock, Arkansas.

She may have ended up disillusioned about her portrayal in newspapers, magazines, and public opinion polls, but Hillary maintained her enthusiasm for the part of campaigning that allowed her to speak directly with people. At a pleasant lunch in an Italian neighborhood in New York, Hillary traded stories about Arkansas for tales about the Bronx. She said, "See, that's what I wish I could do all day every day."

The turning point in the campaign came after the Democratic National Convention in July 1992, when Governor Clinton was officially chosen as the party's candidate. The convention went well and raised his

Above, candidate Bill Clinton and Hillary go over notes before a speech in Memphis, Tennessee. *Opposite, from right to left,* Hillary Rodham Clinton, presidential candidate Bill Clinton, Tipper Gore, and vice presidential candidate Al Gore board a bus to begin campaigning for the 1992 election.

standings in public opinion polls, but that wasn't enough for him. The Republican National Convention was approaching, and President George Bush would be nominated for reelection. Everyone knew that the speeches at the convention would portray Clinton in the worst possible way. Bill Clinton thought that people might believe what they heard, unless he could get out and meet them personally.

Bill and Hillary boarded a bus, together with the vice presidential candidate, Senator Al Gore, and his wife, Tipper. They traveled thousands of miles together, boosting their support among voters. Hillary and

Tipper became close friends, and that friendship helped sustain Hillary during the rest of the campaign.

Speakers at the Republican Convention did indeed speak harshly against Bill Clinton, but the worst criticism was aimed at Hillary. As it turned out, however, the attacks against her backfired. The American public wanted to hear about issues that directly concerned them—issues such as the faltering economy, not attacks against Hillary Clinton. Bill Clinton's standing in the polls continued to climb.

Hillary's most important role in her husband's campaign for president was probably the one she played behind the scenes. Many friends say she's tougher and more decisive than Bill, and much better organized. Hillary is especially good at solving problems and shaping plans. Bill tests many of his ideas out on her first.

She also helped with some of his speeches. During the campaign, Clinton tended to cram more detail into his speeches than most listeners were willing to follow. Hillary convinced him to be more concise in his arguments. A skilled debater herself, she helped Bill prepare for the three televised presidential debates. And Hillary was the *only* person able to see that Bill got enough rest. Left on his own, he tended to stay up most of the night talking with people.

If a weakness emerged in the campaign operation, Hillary often pointed it out and found ways to correct

At the governor's mansion in Little Rock, Arkansas, Hillary addresses a group of cancer survivors during a "Celebration of Life" picnic.

it. She persuaded Bill to appear on the "Arsenio Hall Show," where he played his saxophone. This appearance turned out to be important because it improved his image with young voters.

Talking all night is exactly what Bill Clinton did the night before the November 3, 1992, election. Even though most polls showed that he had a fairly comfortable lead over George Bush, he wouldn't stop campaigning. For 30 straight hours, he crisscrossed the country, speaking and shaking hands, seeking last-minute support. Hillary was at his side. She was exhausted and no doubt felt relieved that the campaign was almost over.

During a campaign stop in Manchester, New Hampshire, the Clintons listen to waitress Maura Johnson as they eat breakfast. They discussed education policy with Johnson after she told them of her ambition to become a teacher.

They returned home to Little Rock early on election day, voted, and then rested—but only briefly. Bill and Chelsea went for a jog together during the afternoon, and he later dropped into a neighborhood McDonald's for a soft drink and conversation with customers. During the long evening, the Clinton family watched the election results on television. Bill Clinton was winning state after state.

In front of the Old Statehouse in Little Rock, 16 blocks had been barricaded. Tens of thousands of

Arkansans, along with about 4,000 journalists, began gathering early, in spite of a cold, steady drizzle. Around 10:00 that evening, when President Bush conceded defeat, the crowd began its wild celebration. They shouted out Bill Clinton's name, anxious for his appearance and his victory speech. And many voices also called a different name: "Hillary! Hillary!"

Bill, Hillary, and Chelsea Clinton finally climbed to the stage in front of the crowd, along with Al Gore and his family. Several more minutes of even louder cheering followed.

When the time came for the president-elect's acceptance speech, Hillary handed him the notecards and he stepped to the microphone. His voice was almost entirely gone from the weeks of campaign speeches, but he managed a few hoarse words, including, "I want to begin this night by thanking my family, my wife, without whom I would not be here tonight and who I believe will be one of the greatest First Ladies in the history of this republic."

The celebration continued for hours. Bill and Hillary danced together on the stage to the old rock tune that had become the official campaign song, Fleetwood Mac's "Don't Stop Thinking about Tomorrow." Even as she danced and hugged and rejoiced, Hillary was probably also doing just that—thinking about tomorrow.

Hillary speaks at her former high school Maine South in Park Ridge, Illinois, during a 1992 campaign visit.

7
Free to Be Herself?

Within two weeks of the election, Bill Clinton visited President George Bush at the White House, and television cameras rolled. But Hillary Rodham Clinton gave the first postelection speech by a Clinton in Washington.

She chose the Children's Defense Fund annual dinner to make her first public remarks after her husband's dramatic victory. People were already saying that in Hillary, children had finally found a spokesperson for their needs. After years of inaction during the administrations of presidents Ronald Reagan and George Bush, children's issues would finally get the attention they deserve.

"All of us have to recognize that we owe our children more than we have been giving them," she said at the

Above, President Bill Clinton is sworn in by Chief Justice William H. Rehnquist as Hillary looks on. *Opposite,* President Clinton helps the First Lady with her coat at the New England inaugural ball.

dinner. "I hope and I trust that together all of us will do all we can to make sure no child is left behind."

During the months between the election and the inauguration, Hillary enjoyed more freedom to speak up and be herself in public than she had during the campaign. No one doubted that she would remain an activist, but it was not clear at first what, exactly, Hillary would do. How would she juggle her roles of First Lady, wife, mother, and lawyer?

74

One of the first clues about Hillary's role came when her husband met with Democratic leaders in Congress. Hillary sat in on this meeting. When asked about it by reporters, President-elect Clinton said, "She stayed the whole time, talked a lot. She knew more than we did about some things." Apparently, others at the meeting agreed. Political analyst David S. Broder wrote, "So the country is clearly on notice that the first member of the baby-boom generation to become First Lady is going to rewrite the rules for the office."

On January 25, 1993, less than a week after his inauguration, President Clinton appointed Hillary to head his Task Force on National Health Care Reform. He said that he appointed her because "she's better at organizing and leading people from a complex beginning to a certain end than anybody I've ever worked with in my life." He added that the nation would soon find that "we have a First Lady of many talents."

According to the *New York Times*, Hillary Rodham Clinton is the first First Lady to be assigned such an important position. She is also the first to occupy an office in the West Wing of the White House, near the president and other senior White House advisers. First Ladies have always had their offices in the East Wing and have employed social secretaries rather than policy experts. President Clinton said he believed that the best way to demonstrate to the American people that he was serious about health care was to put his wife in charge, thus staking both his credibility and hers on achieving results. Hillary will not be paid for her work on behalf of the Clinton administration.

Hillary said she was surprised that anyone might find it unusual that she will be combining the traditional role of First Lady with her work as head of the President's Task Force on National Health Care Reform. She sees herself as no different from "every woman who gets up in the morning and gets breakfast for her family and goes off to a job of any sort where she assumes a different role for the hours she's at work, who runs out at lunch to buy material for a costume for her daughter or to buy invitations for a party that she's going to have, and after work goes and picks up her children and then maybe goes out with her husband: our lives *are* a mixture of these different roles. I'm still always a little bit amazed at how big an issue this is for people because if they will just stop and think, this is what women do."

Many historians say that, as a symbol of the national debate over the role of women in society, Hillary is likely to evoke mixed reactions. Thomas Cronin, a political science professor at Colorado College and an expert on the presidency, said, "She's a pacesetter, and I kind of like it." But he was quick to add, "She's walking on the edge."

The First Lady addresses supporters of the Children's Defense Fund, an organization that she has supported since college.

Two staff reporters for the *Wall Street Journal* wrote that "she shatters all the precedents." Hillary Rodham Clinton has no example to follow. Instead, she's shaping a new role for First Ladies.

On February 4, 1993, Hillary made her first appearance on Capitol Hill for official meetings with Senate leaders of both political parties. Her visit was described as "seismic," meaning that it had the effect of an earthquake. Washington, D.C., has traditionally been a stronghold of white, male power, and it is a city where protocol—a strict code of behavior—is almost as important as policy. Some lawmakers grumbled about a First Lady with a briefcase, but those who met with Hillary Rodham Clinton were impressed with her grasp of health-care issues.

President Clinton announces that the First Lady, Hillary Rodham Clinton, will be the chairperson of the President's Task Force on National Health Care Reform.

The *New York Times* talked about "the First Lady's stunning debut as the most openly empowered presidential wife in American history," and called her trip to Capitol Hill "extraordinary for a First Lady." Donna Shalala, the secretary of the Department of Health and Human Services, believes that Hillary Clinton is taking a huge risk by taking on a political role with such high visibility. But she says that this First Lady "represents a different generational experience [than previous First Ladies]. She's on the cutting edge of that and it's very tricky, because she's on the borderline between a more traditional role and this new role for women. Twenty years from now we won't think twice."

What is a First Lady to Hillary Clinton? "A partner," she answers. "A partner who represents for all of us a view of who her husband is, as well as a symbol of women's concerns and interests at a particular time."

But partnership is not everything to her. "You are who you are," she says, "not who you're married to. At the core is your own identity, and the challenge is to discover who *you* are." With a hint of a smile, she adds, "And I know who I am."

Peachtree City Library
201 Willowbend Road
Peachtree City, Ga. 30269